Born in 1959

by

Kerry Butters.

Born in 1959

Millennium:	**2nd millennium**
Centuries:	19th century – **20th century** – 21st century
Decades:	1920s 1930s 1940s – **1950s** – 1960s 1970s 1980s
Years:	1956 1957 1958 – **1959** – 1960 1961 1962

1959 (MCMLIX) was a common year starting on Thursday (dominical letter D) of the Gregorian calendar, the 1959th year of the Common Era (CE) and *Anno Domini* (AD) designations, the 959th year of the 2nd millennium, the 59th year of the 20th century, and the 10th and last year of the 1950s decade.

Contents

Events

January

- January 1
  - Cultivars of plants named after this date must be named in a modern language, not in Latin.
  - Cuba: Fulgencio Batista flees Havana when the forces of Fidel Castro advance.
- January 2
  - CBS Radio discontinues four soap operas: *Backstage Wife*, *Our Gal Sunday*, *The Road of Life*, and *This is Nora Drake*.
  - Castro's troops approach Havana.
  - The Soviet Union successfully launches the Luna 1 spacecraft from Baikonur Cosmodrome.
- January 3
  - The island of Addu in the Maldives declares independence.
  - Alaska is admitted as the 49th U.S. state.
- January 4
  - In Cuba, rebel troops led by Che Guevara and Camilo Cienfuegos enter the city of Havana.

- In Léopoldville, at least 49 people are killed during clashes between the police and participants of a meeting of the Abako Party.
- January 6
  - Fidel Castro arrives in Havana.
  - The International Maritime Organization is inaugurated.
- January 7 – The United States recognizes the new Cuban government of Fidel Castro.
- January 8 – Charles de Gaulle is inaugurated as the first president of the French Fifth Republic.
- January 10 – The Soviet government recognizes the new Castro government.
- January 11 – The Confédération Mondiale des Activités Subaquatiques is founded in Monaco.
- January 12
  - The Caves of Nerja are discovered in Spain.
  - Motown Records is founded by Berry Gordy, Jr.
- January 13 – Cuban communists execute 71 supporters of Fulgencio Batista.
- January 15 – The Soviet Union conducts its first census after World War II.
- January 21 – The European Court of Human Rights is established.
- January 22 – Knox Mine Disaster: Water breaches the River Slope Mine in Port Griffith, Pennsylvania near Pittston, Pennsylvania; 12 miners are killed.
- January 25 – Pope John XXIII announces that the Second Vatican Council will be convened in Rome.
- January 29 – Walt Disney releases his 16th animated film, *Sleeping Beauty* in Beverly Hills. It is Disney's first animated film to be shown in 70mm and modern 6-track stereophonic sound. Also on the program is Disney's new

live-action short subject *Grand Canyon*, which uses the music of Ferde Grofé's *Grand Canyon Suite*. *Grand Canyon* wins an Oscar for Best Documentary Short.

- January 30 – Danish passenger/cargo ship MS *Hans Hedtoft*, returning to Copenhagen after its maiden voyage to Greenland, strikes an iceberg and sinks off the Greenland coast with the loss of all 95 on board.

January 3 Alaska

February

February 3: Crash kills musicians and pilot.

- February 1 – A referendum in Switzerland turns down female suffrage.
- February 2 – Nine ski hikers mysteriously perish in the northern Ural Mountains in the Dyatlov Pass incident and are all found dead a few weeks later.
- February 3
  - A chartered plane transporting musicians Buddy Holly, Ritchie Valens and The Big Bopper with pilot Roger Peterson goes down in foggy conditions near Clear Lake, Iowa, killing all four on board. The tragedy is later termed "The Day the Music Died",

- popularized in Don McLean's 1971 song "American Pie".
  - American Airlines Flight 320, a Lockheed L-188 Electra from Chicago crashes into the East River on approach to New York City's LaGuardia Airport, killing 65 of the 73 people on board.
- February 6 – At Cape Canaveral, Florida, the first successful test firing of a Titan intercontinental ballistic missile is accomplished.
- February 9 – Yugoslavia and Spain set trade relations (not diplomatic ones).
- February 13 – TAT-2, AT&T's second transatlantic telephone cable goes into operation.
- February 16
  - Fidel Castro becomes Premier of Cuba.
  - A blizzard causes a massive power outage in Newfoundland.
- February 17 – Vanguard 2, the first weather satellite, is launched to measure cloud cover for the United States Navy.
- February 18
  - Jesús Sosa Blanco, a colonel in the Cuban army of Fulgencio Batista, is executed in Cuba after being convicted of committing 108 murders for Batista.
  - Women in Nepal vote for the first time.
- February 19 – The United Kingdom decides to grant Cyprus its independence.
- February 20 – The Canadian Government cancels the Avro Canada CF-105 Arrow interceptor aircraft project.
- February 22 – Lee Petty wins the first Daytona 500 at Daytona International Speedway.

March

- March 1
  - The USS *Tuscaloosa*, USS *New Orleans*, USS *Tennessee* and USS *West Virginia* are struck from the Naval Vessel Register.
  - Archbishop Makarios returns to Cyprus from exile.
- March 2 – Recording sessions for the album *Kind of Blue* by Miles Davis take place at Columbia's 30th Street Studio in New York City.
- March 8 – The Marx Brothers make their last television appearance, in *The Incredible Jewel Robbery*.
- March 9 – The Barbie doll debuts.
- March 10 – A Tibetan uprising against 10 years of Chinese rule erupts in Lhasa.
- March 11
  - *Een beetje* by Teddy Scholten (music by Dick Schallies, text by Willy van Hemert) wins the Eurovision Song Contest for the Netherlands.
  - *A Raisin in the Sun* by Lorraine Hansberry opens on Broadway.
- March 17 – Tenzin Gyatso, 14th Dalai Lama, flees Tibet.
- March 18 – American President Dwight D. Eisenhower signs a bill allowing for Hawaiian statehood.
- March 19 – Two other islands join Addu in the United Suvadive Republic (abolished September 1963), in the Maldives Islands.
- March 31
  - Busch Gardens in Tampa, Florida opens.
  - The Dalai Lama is granted asylum in India.

April

- April 6 – The 31st Academy Awards ceremony is held.
- April 8 – The Inter-American Development Bank (IADB) is established.
- April 9 – NASA announces its selection of seven military pilots to become the first U.S. astronauts (later known as the *Mercury Seven*).
- April 10 – Crown Prince Akihito of Japan marries Shōda Michiko, the first commoner to marry into the Imperial House of Japan.
- April 22 – Recording sessions for the influential jazz album Kind of Blue by Miles Davis take place at Columbia's 30th Street Studio in New York City.
- April 25 – The Saint Lawrence Seaway linking the Great Lakes and the Atlantic Ocean officially opens to shipping.
- April 27 – National People's Congress elects Liu Shaoqi as Chairman of the People's Republic of China, as a successor of Mao Zedong.

May

- May
  - The first Ten Tors event is held in Dartmoor.
  - Import tariffs are lifted in the United Kingdom.
- May 2 – 1959 FA Cup Final: Nottingham Forest defeats Luton Town 2–1.
- May 18 – The National Liberation Committee of Côte d'Ivoire is launched in Conakry, Guinea.

- May 21 – *Gypsy: A Musical Fable*, starring Ethel Merman in her last new musical, opens on Broadway and runs for 702 performances
- May 24 – British Empire Day is renamed Commonwealth Day.
- May 28 – Two monkeys, Able and Miss Baker are the first living beings to successfully return to Earth from space aboard the flight Jupiter AM-18.

June

- June 3
  - Singapore becomes a self-governing crown colony of Britain with Lee Kuan Yew as Prime Minister.
  - Real Madrid beats Stade Reims 2–0 at Neckarstadion, Stuttgart and wins the 1958–59 European Cup (football).
- June 5 – A new government of the State of Singapore is sworn in by Sir William Goode. Two former ministers are re-elected to the Legislative Assembly.
- June 8 – The USS *Barbero* and United States Postal Service attempt the delivery of mail via Missile Mail.
- June 9 – The USS *George Washington* is launched as the first submarine to carry ballistic missiles.
- June 14
  - Disneyland Monorail System, the first daily operating monorail system in the Western Hemisphere, opens to the public in Anaheim, California.
  - A 3-front revolutionary invasion by air and sea takes place in the Dominican Republic, consisting of exiles aided by Fidel Castro and the Venezuelan government, whose objective is to overthrow dictator Rafael

Trujillo. Within a few days most are captured and executed. Only four are released by the government. Trujillo is killed less than two years later by men partly inspired by the deaths of the 1959 revolutionaries.

- June 18 – The film *The Nun's Story*, based on the best-selling novel, is released. Audrey Hepburn stars as the title character; she later says that this is her favorite film role. The film is a box-office hit, and is nominated for several Oscars.
- June 23
  - Seán Lemass becomes the third Taoiseach of Ireland.
  - Convicted Manhattan Project spy Klaus Fuchs is released after only nine years in a British prison and allowed to emigrate to Dresden, East Germany where he resumes a scientific career.
- June 25 – A KH-1 *Corona*, believed to be the first operational spy satellite, is launched as science mission "Discoverer 4" from Vandenberg Air Force Base aboard a Thor-Agena rocket.
- June 26
  - Elizabeth II (Queen of Canada) and United States President Dwight Eisenhower open the Saint Lawrence Seaway.
  - *Darby O'Gill and the Little People*, a film based on H. T. Kavanagh's short stories, is released in the U.S. by the Walt Disney Company two days after a world premiere in Ireland.
- June 30 – Twenty-one students are killed and more than a hundred injured when an American North American F-100 Super Sabre jet crashes into Miamori Elementary School on the island of Okinawa. The pilot ejected before the plane struck the school.

July

- July 1 – Australia's longest running children's TV series, *Mr. Squiggle*, first airs on ABC Television.
- July 2 – Prince Albert of Belgium marries Italian Donna Paola Ruffo di Calabria.
- July 4 – With the admission of Alaska as the 49th U.S. state earlier in the year, the 49-star flag of the United States debuts in Philadelphia.
- July 7 – At 14:28 UT Venus occults the star Regulus. The rare event (which will next occur on October 1, 2044) is used to determine the diameter of Venus and the structure of Venus' atmosphere.
- July 14 – Groups of Kurdish and communist militias rebel in Kirkuk, Iraq against the central government.
- July 15 – A strike occurs against the United States' steel industry.
- July 17 – The first skull of Australopithecus is discovered by Louis Leakey and his wife Mary Leakey in the Olduvai Gorge of Tanzania.
- July 22 – A Kumamoto University medical research group studying Minamata disease concludes that it is caused by mercury.
- July 24 – At the opening of the American National Exhibition in Moscow, United States Vice President Richard Nixon and USSR Premier Nikita Khrushchev engage in the "Kitchen Debate".
- July 25 – The SR.N1 hovercraft crosses the English Channel from Calais to Dover in just over 2 hours, on the 50th anniversary of Louis Blériot's first crossing by heavier-than-air craft.

August

- August 4 – Martial law is declared in Laos.
- August 7
  - Explorer program: The United States launches Explorer 6 from the Atlantic Missile Range in Cape Canaveral, Florida.
  - United States: The Roseburg, Oregon blast kills 14 and causes $12 million worth of damage.
- August 8 – A flood in Taiwan kills 2,000.
- August 14 – Explorer 6 sends the first picture of Earth from orbit.
- August 15 – Cyprus gains independence.
- August 17
  - The 1959 Hebgen Lake earthquake in southwest Montana kills 28.
  - Columbia Records releases Miles Davis' groundbreaking album, *Kind of Blue*.
- August 19 – The Central Treaty Organization (CENTO) is established.
- August 21 – Hawaii is admitted as the 50th U.S. state.
- August 24 – Cyprus joins the United Nations.
- August 26 – The original Mini designed by Sir Alec Issigonis is launched.

September

- September 14 – Luna 2 becomes the first man-made object to crash on the Moon.

- September 15 – September 28 – USSR Premier Nikita Khrushchev and his wife tour the United States, at the invitation of U.S. President Dwight David Eisenhower.
- September 16 – The Xerox 914, the first plain paper copier, is introduced to the public.
- September 17
  - The first *Navy Navigation Satellite System* Transit 1A is launched but fails to reach orbit.
  - The Hypersonic North American X-15 Research Vehicle, piloted by Scott Crossfield, makes its first powered flight at Edwards Air Force Base, California.
- September 23 – The *M/S Princess of Tasmania*, (Australia's first passenger RO/RO diesel ferry), makes its maiden voyage across the Bass Strait.
- September 25 – Ceylon's prime minister S. W. R. D. Bandaranaike is assassinated.
- September 26
  - Typhoon Vera hits central Honshū, Japan, killing an estimated 5,098, injuring another 38,921, and leaving 1,533,000 homeless. Most of the victims and damage are centered in the Nagoya area.
  - The first official large unit action of the Vietnam War takes place, when two companies of the ARVN 23d Division are ambushed by a well-organized Vietcong force of several hundred, identified as the "2d Liberation Battalion".
- September 30 – Soviet Union leader Nikita Khrushchev meets Mao Zedong in Beijing.
-

September 13: Luna 2.

October

- October 1 – The 10th anniversary of the People's Republic of China is celebrated with pomp across the country.
- October 2 – Rod Serling's classic anthology series *The Twilight Zone* premieres on CBS.
- October 7 – The U.S.S.R. probe *Luna 3* sends back the first ever photos of the far side of the Moon.
- October 12 – At the national APRA Congress in Peru, a group of leftist radicals is expelled from the party; they later form APRA Rebelde.
- October 13 – The United States launches Explorer 7.
- October 21 – In New York City, the Solomon R. Guggenheim Museum (designed by Frank Lloyd Wright) opens to the public.
- October 29 – First appearance of Astérix the Gaul.
- October 31 – Riots break out in the Belgian Congo.

November

- November 1 – In Rwanda, Hutu politician Dominique Mbonyumutwa is beaten up by Tutsi forces, leading to a period of violence known as the wind of destruction.
- November 2 – At a ceremony near Toddington, British Minister of Transport Ernest Marples opens the first section

of the M1 Motorway, between Watford and Crick, along with two spur motorways, the M45 and M10. Three decades of large scale motorway construction follow, leading to the rapid expansion of the UK motorway network.

- November 12 – The Warner Bros. religious epic *The Miracle*, very loosely based on the 1911 stage pantomime *Das Mirakel*, is released. It is a critical and financial bomb.
- November 15 – The Clutter family of Holcomb, Kansas is brutally murdered, inspiring Truman Capote's *In Cold Blood*.
- November 18 – MGM's widescreen, multimillion-dollar, Technicolor version of *Ben-Hur*, starring Charlton Heston, is released and becomes the studio's greatest hit up to that time. It is critically acclaimed and eventually wins 11 Academy Awards – a record held until 1998, when 1997's *Titanic* becomes the first film to equal the record. To the present day, the 1959 *Ben-Hur* remains the last MGM film to win a Best Picture Oscar, though *Doctor Zhivago*, another MGM film, was nominated in 1965.
- November 20 – The Declaration of the Rights of the Child is adopted by the United Nations.

December

- December 1 – Cold War – Antarctic Treaty: 12 countries, including the United States and the Soviet Union, sign a landmark treaty, which sets aside Antarctica as a scientific preserve and bans military activity on that continent (the first arms control agreement established during the Cold War).

- December 2 – Malpasset Dam in southern France collapses and water flows over the town of Fréjus, killing 412.
- December 8 – The *Mona*, a lifeboat based at Broughty Ferry in Scotland, capsizes during a rescue attempt, with the loss of 8 lives.
- December 14 – Makarios III is selected the first president of Cyprus.

Date unknown

- Pantyhose is introduced by Glen Raven Mills.
- The Workers World Party is founded by Sam Marcy.
- The first known human with HIV dies in the Congo.
- The current (as of 2006) design of the Japanese 10 yen coin is put into circulation.
- The Caspian tiger becomes extinct in Iran.
- The Henney Kilowatt goes on sale in the United States, becoming the first mass-produced electric car in almost three decades.
- Erving Goffman publishes his seminal study in sociology, *The Presentation of Self in Everyday Life*.
- The Daytona International Speedway is built.
- The iconic 1959 Cadillac is introduced, with tailfin wars peaking that had begun in 1948.

Births

January

Keith Olbermann

Larry McReynolds

- January 1 – Azali Assoumani, President of the Comoros
- January 2 – Joe Bevilacqua, American producer, director, writer, actor
- January 4
  - Vanity, Canadian singer and actress (d. 2016)
  - Yoshitomo Nara, Japanese artist
- January 5 – Clancy Brown, American actor
- January 6 – Andrew Johnson, English artist
- January 9
  - Rigoberta Menchú, Guatemalan recipient of the Nobel Peace Prize
  - Mark Martin, American NASCAR driver

- January 10 – Larry McReynolds, American Fox Sports commentator
- January 12
  - Per Gessle, Swedish singer-songwriter
  - Roxette, guitarist
- January 16 – Sade, Nigerian-born singer
- January 17
  - Susanna Hoffs, American rock vocalist
  - Momoe Yamaguchi, Japanese singer
- January 21
  - Alex McLeish, Nottingham Forest player
  - Paulo Miklos, Brazilian singer and actor
- January 22 – Linda Blair, American actress
- January 24 – Vic Reeves, English comedian
- January 27 – Keith Olbermann, American news anchor and sportscaster
- January 29 – Mike Foligno, Canadian ice hockey player
- January 30 – Jody Watley, African-American singer
- January 31 – Kelly Moore, American race car driver

February

Kyle MacLachlan

- February 2
  - Jari Tervo, Finnish author
  - Hella von Sinnen, German TV-entertainer

- February 3 – UliUli Fifita, Tongan professional Wrestler aka(Haku/Meng)
- February 4
  - Pamelyn Ferdin, American former child actress; animal rights activist
  - Raquel Morell, Mexican actress
  - Lawrence Taylor, American football player
- February 5 – Jennifer Granholm, Canadian-American politician, 47th Governor of Michigan (2003–2011)
- February 6
  - Pat Bullard, Canadian game show host, comedian and writer
  - Ken Nelson, English record producer
- February 7 – Vladimír Havlík, Czech action artist
- February 10 – Dennis Gentry, American football player
- February 14 – Renée Fleming, American soprano
- February 16 – John McEnroe, American tennis player
- February 18 – Jayne Atkinson, English-born American film, theatre and television actress
- February 22 – Kyle MacLachlan, American actor
- February 25 – Renee M. Borges, Indian ecologist
- February 26 – Rolando Blackman, Panamanian basketball player

March

Jens Stoltenberg

Matthew Modine

Jaime Augusto Zobel de Ayala II

- March 1 – Nick Griffin, British politician
- March 4
  - Rick Ardon, Australian news presenter
  - Irina Strakhova, Russian race walker
- March 5 – Mike Byster, American mathematician, mental calculator and math educator
- March 6
  - Tom Arnold, American actor and comedian
  - Jaime Augusto Zobel de Ayala II, Spanish Filipino businessman
  - Lars Larson, American conservative talk show host
- March 8
  - Lester Holt, American television journalist and news anchor
  - Aidan Quinn, Irish-American actor
- March 9
  - Giovanni di Lorenzo, German-Italian journalist and talk show host

- Takaaki Kajita, Japanese nuclear physicist, recipient of the Nobel Prize in Physics
- March 10 – Mike Wallace, American race car driver
- March 11 – Dejan Stojanović, Serbian-American poet, writer, essayist and businessman
- March 15
  - Harold Baines, American baseball player
  - Fabio Lanzoni, Italian fashion model and actor
- March 16
  - Flavor Flav, American rapper
  - Jens Stoltenberg, 27th Prime Minister of Norway
- March 17
  - Danny Ainge, American basketball player, coach and baseball player
  - Ken Lo, Hong Kong actor and member of the Jackie Chan Stunt Team
- March 18
  - Luc Besson, French film producer, writer and director
  - Irene Cara, African-American singer
- March 20
  - Steve Borden, American wrestler
  - Richard Drummie, English guitarist and composer (Go West)
  - Steve McFadden, British actor
- March 21 – Nobuo Uematsu, Japanese composer
- March 22 – Matthew Modine, American actor
- March 23
  - Kazue Ikura, Japanese voice actress
  - Catherine Keener, American actress
- March 27 – Jun'ichi Sugawara, Japanese voice actor
- March 28 – Laura Chinchilla, President of Costa Rica
- March 29 – Barry Blanchard, Canadian mountaineer

- March 30 – Andrew Bailey, Executive Director Banking and Chief Cashier at the Bank of England
- March 31 – Markus Hediger, Swiss writer and translator

April

David Hyde Pierce

Emma Thompson

Robert Smith

Sean Bean

Stephen Harper

- April 2 – Badou Zaki, Moroccan football player and manager
- April 3 – David Hyde Pierce, American actor
- April 10 – Brian Setzer, American rock guitarist and singer
- April 11 – Ana María Polo, Cuban-born judge and television personality
- April 14 – Steve Byrnes, American motorsports broadcaster (d. 2015)
- April 15
  - Fruit Chan, Hong Kong film director
  - Ray Neufeld, Canadian ice hockey player
  - Emma Thompson, English actress
  - Thomas F. Wilson, American actor
- April 16 – Alison Ramsay, Scottish field hockey player
- April 17 – Sean Bean, British actor
- April 20 – Clint Howard, American actor and producer

- April 21 – Robert Smith, British rock musician (The Cure)
- April 22
  - Terry Francona, American baseball player and manager
  - Ryan Stiles, American comedian
- April 24 – Paula Yates, British television presenter (d. 2000)
- April 25 – Tony Phillips, American baseball player (d. 2016)
- April 27 – Sheena Easton, Scottish singer
- April 30 – Stephen Harper, 22nd Prime Minister of Canada

May

Brian Williams

Rupert Everett

- May 2 – Alan Best, Canadian animation director and producer

- May 3
  - Uma Bharti, Chief Minister of Madhya Pradesh
  - Ben Elton, British comedian and writer
- May 5
  - Peter Molyneux, British game programmer
  - Steve Stevens, American guitarist
  - Brian Williams, American news anchor
- May 9 – János Áder, President of Hungary
- May 10 – Victoria Rowell, American actress
- May 12 – Ving Rhames, American actor
- May 14 – Patrick Bruel, French singer
- May 15 – Andrew Eldritch, British singer/songwriter
- May 17
  - Marcelo Loffreda, Argentine rugby player and coach
  - Jim Nantz, American sports announcer
- May 19 – Nicole Brown Simpson, American ex-wife of O. J. Simpson and murder victim (d. 1994)
- May 20 – Israel Kamakawiwoʻole, American singer (d. 1997)
- May 21
  - Brian Lenihan, Irish politician (d. 2011)
  - Loretta Lynch, United States Attorney General
- May 22
  - David Blatt, Israeli-American professional basketball player and coach
  - Morrissey, British singer
- May 23 – Bob Mortimer, English comedian
- May 24 – Pelle Lindbergh, Swedish-born hockey player (d. 1985)
- May 27 – Katherine Lanpher, American journalist
- May 28 – Steve Strange, Welsh singer (Visage)

- May 29 – Rupert Everett, British actor

June

Hugh Laurie

Christian Wulff

- June 6 – Paul Germain, American television screenwriter and producer
- June 7 – Mike Pence, 50th Governor of Indiana and 2016 GOP vice presidential nominee under Donald Trump
- June 8 – Bernard White, Sri Lankan-born American actor, screenwriter and film director
- June 9 – Miles O'Brien, American television news anchor, pilot
- June 10
  - Carlo Ancelotti, Italian football player and manager
  - Eliot Spitzer, American politician and former governor of New York
- June 11
  - Hugh Laurie, British actor and comedian

- o Magnum T.A., American professional wrestler
- June 12 – John Linnell, American singer-songwriter
- June 13 – Klaus Iohannis, President of Romania
- June 14 – Marcus Miller, American bassist
- June 15 – Eileen Davidson, American actress and author
- June 16 – The Ultimate Warrior, American professional wrestler (d. 2014)
- June 17
  - o Ulrike Richter, German swimmer
  - o Kazuki Yao, Japanese voice actor
- June 19 – Christian Wulff, Federal President of Germany
- June 22
  - o Wayne Federman, American comedian, actor, and author
  - o Ed Viesturs, American mountaineer
- June 26 – Mark McKinney, Canadian actor and comedian
- June 28 – John Shelley, British illustrator
- June 30 – Vincent D'Onofrio, American actor

July

Susana Martinez

Kevin Spacey

- July 3 – Julie Burchill, British journalist
- July 5 – Marc Cohn, American singer-songwriter
- July 6 – Richard Dacoury, French basketball player
- July 7
  - Barbara Krause, German swimmer
  - Ben Linder, American engineer (d. 1987)
- July 9
  - Jim Kerr, Scottish rock singer (Simple Minds)
  - Kevin Nash, American professional wrestler
- July 11
  - Richie Sambora, American musician
  - Suzanne Vega, American singer
- July 14 – Susana Martinez, American politician, Governor of New Mexico
- July 16 – Gary Anderson, American football player
- July 17 – Margaret Becker, American Christian singer
- July 18 – Mel Purcell, American tennis player
- July 19 – Juan J. Campanella, Argentinian filmmaker
- July 25 – Anatoly Onoprienko, Ukrainian serial killer (d. 2013)
- July 26
  - Rick Bragg, American journalist
  - Kevin Spacey, American actor
- July 27 – Hugh Green, American football player
- July 29
  - Sanjay Dutt, Indian actor
  - Ruud Janssen, Dutch artist

August

Rosanna Arquette

Magic Johnson

- August 3 – Koichi Tanaka, Japanese scientist, recipient of the Nobel Prize in Chemistry
- August 4 – Robbin Crosby, American rock guitarist (Ratt) (d. 2002)
- August 5 – Pete Burns, British singer (Dead or Alive)
- August 6 – Rajendra Singh Indian water conservationist, Magsaysay Award (2001)
- August 10 – Rosanna Arquette, American actress
- August 11
  - Gustavo Cerati, Argentinian singer
  - Yoshiaki Murakami, Japanese investor
- August 13 – Danny Bonaduce, American actor and disc jockey
-

- August 14
  - Marcia Gay Harden, American actress
  - Magic Johnson, American basketball player
- August 15 – Scott Altman, American astronaut
- August 17
  - Sakamoto Chika, Japanese voice actress and singer
  - Jonathan Franzen, American author
  - David Koresh, American spiritualist, leader of the Branch Davidian religious cult (d. 1993)
  - Brad Wellman, American baseball player
- August 19 – Anthony Sowell, convicted serial killer and rapist
- August 21 – Jim McMahon, American football player
- August 25 – Sönke Wortmann, German film director
- August 26 – Stan Van Gundy, American basketball coach
- August 27
  - Juan Fernando Cobo, Colombian artist
  - Jürgen Becker, German cabaret artist and actor
- August 29
  - Rebecca De Mornay, American actress
  - Stephen Wolfram, British scientist
- August 30 – Mark 'Jacko' Jackson, Australian rules footballer and actor
- August 31 – Tony DeFranco, Canadian singer

September

Guy Laliberté

Jason Alexander

- September 1 – Kenny Mayne, American sportscaster
- September 2 – Guy Laliberté, Canadian Cirque du Soleil founder
- September 4
  - Kevin Harrington, Australian actor
  - Armin Kogler, Austrian ski jumper
- September 8
  - Daler Nazarov, Tajik composer, singer, and actor
  - Saeko Shimazu, Japanese voice actress
- September 10 – Michael Earl, American puppeteer (d. 2015)
- September 12 – Sigmar Gabriel, German politician
- September 14
  - Mary Crosby, American actress
  - Morten Harket, Norwegian rock singer (A-ha)
  - Haviland Morris, American actress
- September 15 – Mike Reiss, American television comedy writer
- September 17 – Charles Lawson, Irish actor
- September 18
  - Kirk Fogg, American actor, game show host and singer
  - Sérgio Britto, Brazilian singer and keyboardist

- September 21 – Dave Coulier, American actor and comedian
- September 23 – Jason Alexander, American actor and comedian
- September 28 – Dantes Tsitsi, Nauruan politician
- September 29 – Benjamin Sehene, Rwandan writer
- September 30 – Ettore Messina, Italian basketball coach

October

Simon Cowell

Sarah, Duchess of York

"Weird Al" Yankovic

Evo Morales

- October 1
  - Brian P. Cleary, American humorist, author, poet
  - Youssou N'Dour, Senegalese singer
- October 3
  - Fred Couples, American golfer
  - Greg Proops, American comedian
  - Jack Wagner, American actor
- October 4 – Chris Lowe, British musician
- October 5 – David Shannon, American writer and illustrator
- October 7
  - Simon Cowell, English music producer and television talent show judge
  - Lourdes Flores, Peruvian politician
- October 8
  - Nick Bakay, American actor, producer, and screenwriter
  - Brad Byers, American entertainer
  - Gavin Friday, Irish singer-songwriter, actor, and producer (Virgin Prunes)
  - Erik Gundersen, Danish motorcycle racer
  - Mike Morgan, American baseball player and coach
  - Carlos I. Noriega, Peruvian-American colonel and astronaut

- October 9
  - Michael Paré, American actor
  - Boris Nemtsov, Russian politician (d. 2015)
- October 10 – Kirsty MacColl, British singer and songwriter (d. 2000)
- October 13 – Marie Osmond, American singer
- October 15
  - Emeril Lagasse, American chef and restaurant owner
  - Sarah, Duchess of York, British Princess and former wife of Prince Andrew, Duke of York
- October 17 – Richard Roeper, American film critic
- October 21 – Ken Watanabe, Japanese actor
- October 22 – Arto Salminen, Finnish writer (d. 2005)
- October 23
  - Nancy Grace, American television host
  - "Weird Al" Yankovic, American singer and parodist
  - Sam Raimi, American producer, writer and director
- October 25 – Chrissy Amphlett, Australian rock singer (d. 2013)
- October 26 – Evo Morales, President of Bolivia
- October 27 – Rick Carlisle, American basketball coach
- October 29 – John Magufuli, President of Tanzania
- October 31 – Neal Stephenson, American writer

November

Bryan Adams

Allison Janney

Sean Young

- November 2 – Saïd Aouita, Moroccan athlete
- November 5 – Bryan Adams, Canadian singer and photographer
- November 6 – Nobuo Tobita, Japanese voice actor
- November 7 – Billy Gillispie, American basketball coach
- November 8 – Selçuk Yula, Turkish football player and top scorer
- November 9 – Tony Slattery, British comedian and actor
- November 10
    - Linda Cohn, American sports reporter
    - Mackenzie Phillips, American actress
    - Mike McCarthy, American football coach
- November 11 – Christian Schwarzenegger, Swiss legal scientist and professor
- November 14 – Paul McGann, British actor

- November 17 – William R. Moses, American actor
- November 18 – Jimmy Quinn, Northern Irish footballer and football manager
- November 19
  - Jo Bonner, American U.S. Representative for Alabama's 1st congressional district
  - Allison Janney, American actress
- November 20 – Sean Young, American actress
- November 23 – Dominique Dunne, American actress (d. 1982)
- November 24 – Akio Ōtsuka, Japanese voice actor and actor
- November 25 – Charles Kennedy, British politician (d. 2015)
- November 27 – Viktoria Mullova, Russian violinist
- November 28 – Judd Nelson, American actor
- November 29
  - Rahm Emanuel, American politician
  - Platon Lebedev, Russian executive
- November 30 – Lorraine Kelly, British presenter and journalist

December

Satoru Iwata

Val Kilmer

- December 1
  - Billy Childish, English painter, writer and musician
  - Wally Lewis, Australian sport identity
- December 4 – Christa Luding-Rothenburger, German speed skater
- December 6 – Satoru Iwata, Japanese president of Nintendo (d. 2015)
- December 13 – Johnny Whitaker, American actor
- December 14 – Evan Ziporyn, American composer
- December 16
  - Alison LaPlaca, American actress
  - Steve Mattsson, American writer
- December 17 – Gregg Araki, American director
- December 19 – Waise Lee, Hong Kong actor
- December 20 – Stephen Chan Chi Wan, general manager of TVB
- December 21 – Florence Griffith Joyner, African-American athlete (d. 1998)
- December 22 – Bernd Schuster, German footballer and manager
- December 24 – Keith Deller, English darts player
- December 25 – Michael P. Anderson, American Astronaut (d. 2003)
- December 27 – Gerina Dunwich, American author
- December 28 – Ana Torroja, Spanish singer

- December 30 – Tracey Ullman, British-American comedian and actress
- December 31
  ○ Val Kilmer, American actor
  ○ Baron Waqa, Nauruan politician and composer

Date unknown

- Jacki Randall, American artist
- Karl Shuker, British zoologist, crypto-zoologist, and author

Deaths

January

- January 2 – William D. Francis, Australian botanist (b. 1889)
- January 3 – Edwin Muir, Scottish poet, novelist and translator (b. 1887)
- January 8 – Zhang Xi, Chinese politician (b. 1912)
- January 21
  ○ Cecil B. DeMille, American film director (b. 1881)
  ○ Carl Switzer, American actor (b. 1927)
- January 22 – Mike Hawthorn, English race car driver (b. 1929)
- January 26 – MacGillivray Milne, United States Navy Captain and the 27th Governor of American Samoa (b. 1882)
- January 28 – Walter Beall, American baseball player (b. 1899)

February

- February 1 – Frank Shannon, American actor (b. 1874)

- February 3 – Killed in the crash of a private plane:
  - The Big Bopper (J.P. Richardson), American rock singer (b. 1930)
  - Buddy Holly, American rock singer (b. 1936)
  - Roger Peterson, pilot (b. 1937)
  - Ritchie Valens, American rock singer (b. 1941)
- February 3 – Vincent Astor, American philanthropist (b. 1891)
- February 4 – Una O'Connor, Irish actress (b. 1880)
- February 7 – Nap Lajoie, American baseball player (Cleveland Indians) and a member of the MLB Hall of Fame (b. 1874)
- February 11 – Marshall Teague, American race car driver (b. 1922)
- February 12 – George Antheil, American composer (b. 1900)
- February 14 – Baby Dodds, American jazz musician (b. 1898)
- February 15 – Owen Willans Richardson, British physicist, Nobel Prize laureate (b. 1879)
- February 18 – Gago Coutinho, Portuguese aviation pioneer (b. 1869)
- February 20 – Laurence Housman, English playwright and writer (b. 1865)
- February 22 – Helen Parrish, American actress (b. 1924)
- February 23 – Luis Palés Matos, Puerto Rican poet (b. 1898)
- February 26
  - Princess Alexandra, 2nd Duchess of Fife, eldest grandchild of King Edward VII (b. 1891)
  - Selig Suskin, Russian-born Israeli agronomist and early Zionist (b. 1873)

- February 28 – Maxwell Anderson, American screenwriter (b. 1888)

March

- March 1 – Mack Gordon, American composer and lyricist (b. 1904)
- March 2 – Eric Blore, English actor (b. 1887)
- March 3 – Lou Costello, American actor and comedian (b. 1906)
- March 4 – Maxie Long, American athlete (b. 1878)
- March 6 – Fred Stone, American actor (b. 1873)
- March 15 – Lester Young, American jazz saxophonist (b. 1909)
- March 17 – Galaktion Tabidze, Georgian poet (b. 1891)
- March 21 – Edwin Balmer, American science fiction and mystery writer (b. 1883)
- March 25 – Billy Mayerl, English pianist and composer (b. 1902)
- March 26 – Raymond Chandler, American-born novelist (b. 1888)
- March 27 – Grant Withers, American actor (b. 1905)
- March 29 – Barthélemy Boganda, first President of the Central African Republic (b. 1910)
- March 30 – Reginald R. Belknap, United States Navy rear admiral (b. 1871)

April

Frank Lloyd Wright

- April 6 – Leo Aryeh Mayer, Israeli professor and scholar of Islamic art (b. 1895)
- April 8 – Mario de Bernardi, Italian aviator (b. 1893)
- April 9 – Frank Lloyd Wright, American architect (b. 1867)
- April 12 – James Gleason, American actor (b. 1882)
- April 18 – Irving Cummings, American actor (b. 1888)
- April 29 – Kenneth Arthur Noel Anderson, British general (b. 1891)

May

- May 3 – Troy Sanders, American film score composer (b. 1901)
- May 4 – William S. Pye, American admiral (b. 1880)
- May 5 – Carlos Saavedra Lamas, Argentine politician, recipient of the Nobel Peace Prize (b. 1878)
- May 14 – Sidney Bechet, American musician (b. 1897)
- May 16 – Elisha Scott, Irish footballer (b. 1894)
- May 17 – George Albert Smith, English film pioneer (b. 1864)
- May 18
    - Apsley Cherry-Garrard, Antarctic explorer (b. 1886)
    - Enrique Guaita, Argentinian footballer (b. 1910)

- May 20 – Alfred Schütz, Austrian sociologist (b. 1899)
- May 24 – John Foster Dulles, United States Secretary of State (b. 1888)
- May 29 – Ed Walsh, American baseball player (Chicago White Sox) and a member of the MLB Hall of Fame (b. 1881)
- May 30 – Raúl Scalabrini Ortiz, Argentinian journalist (b. 1898)
- May 31 – Ede Zathureczky, Hungarian violinist (b. 1903)

June

Adolf Otto Reinhold Windaus

- June 4 – Charles Vidor, American director (b. 1900)
- June 8 – Pietro Canonica, sculptor (b. 1869)
- June 9
  - Sonnie Hale, British actor and director (b. 1902)
  - Adolf Otto Reinhold Windaus, German chemist, Nobel Prize laureate (b. 1876)
- June 16 – George Reeves, American TV actor (b. 1914)
- June 18 – Ethel Barrymore, American stage & screen actress (b. 1879)
- June 20 – Hitoshi Ashida, Prime Minister of Japan 1948 (b. 1887)
- June 23 – Boris Vian, French writer, poet, singer, and musician (b. 1920)

- June 25 – Charles Starkweather, American spree killer (b. 1938)

July

- July 6 – George Grosz, German artist (b. 1893)
- July 7 – Ernest Newman, English music critic (b. 1868)
- July 9 – Ferenc Talányi, Slovene writer, partisan and painter (b. 1883)
- July 11 – Charlie Parker, English cricketer (b. 1882)
- July 15 – Ernest Bloch, Swiss composer (b. 1880)
- July 17 – Billie Holiday, American singer (b. 1915)
- July 25
  - Yitzhak HaLevi Herzog, Polish-born Chief Rabbi of Ireland, and later of Israel (b. 1888)
  - King Mutara III of Rwanda (b. circa 1912)

August

- August 3 – Herb Byrne, Australian rules footballer (b. 1887)
- August 5 – Edgar Guest, English poet (b. 1881)
- August 6 – Preston Sturges, American film director and writer (b. 1898)
- August 15 – Blind Willie McTell, African-American Piedmont blues singer and guitarist (b. 1901)
- August 16
  - Benny Fields, American singer (b. 1894)
  - William Halsey, Jr., American admiral (b. 1882)
  - Wanda Landowska, Polish harpsichordist (b. 1879)
- August 19
  - Claude Grahame-White, British aviation pioneer (b. 1879)
  - Jacob Epstein, American-born sculptor (b. 1880)

- August 28
  - Raphael Lemkin, international lawyer (b. 1900)
  - Bohuslav Martinů, Czech composer (b. 1890)

September

- September 1 – Jack Norworth, American singer and songwriter (b. 1879)
- September 6
  - Edmund Gwenn, English actor (b. 1877)
  - Kay Kendall, English actress (b. 1927)
- September 7 – Maurice Duplessis, Premier of Quebec (b. 1890)
- September 11 – Paul Douglas, American actor (b. 1907)
- September 13 – Gilbert Adrian, American costume designer (b. 1903)
- September 14 – Wayne Morris, American actor (b. 1914)
- September 17 – Jack Llewelyn Davies, one of the 'Lost Boys' for the Peter Pan book (b. 1894)
- September 25
  - Solomon Bandaranaike, prime minister of Ceylon (b. 1899)
  - Helen Broderick, American actress (b. 1891)
- September 28
  - Rudolf Caracciola, German race car driver (b. 1901)
  - Oscar Griswold, American general (b. 1886)
  - Gerard Hoffnung, German-born English humorist (b. 1925)
  - Vinnie Richards, American tennis player (b. 1903)
- September 30 – Taylor Holmes, American actor (b. 1878)

October

George C. Marshall

- October 6 – Bernard Berenson, American art historian (b. 1865)
- October 7 – Mario Lanza, American tenor (b. 1921)
- October 9 – Shirō Ishii, Japanese microbiologist and lieutenant general of Unit 731 (b. 1892)
- October 11 – Bert Bell, 2nd commissioner of the National Football League (b. 1895)
- October 14 – Errol Flynn, Australian actor (b. 1909)
- October 15 – Stepan Bandera, Ukrainian nationalist leader (b. 1909)
- October 16
  - Minor Hall, American jazz musician (b. 1897)
  - George C. Marshall, United States Secretary of State, recipient of the Nobel Peace Prize (b. 1880)
- October 18 – Boughera El Ouafi, Algerian athlete (b. 1898)
- October 19 – Ebrahim Hakimi, Prime Minister of Iran (b. 1871)
- October 20 – Werner Krauss, German actor (b. 1884)
- October 22 – Joseph Cahill, Australian politician (b. 1891)
- October 28 – Camilo Cienfuegos, Cuban revolutionary (b. 1932)

November

- November 1 – M. K. Thyagaraja Bhagavathar, Tamil film actor and producer (b. 1909)
- November 2 – Michael Considine, Australian politician (b. 1885)
- November 6 – José P. Laurel, Philippine President (b. 1891)
- November 7 – Victor McLaglen, English actor (b. 1886)
- November 8 – Frank S. Land, founder of the Order of DeMolay (b. 1890)
- November 10 – Lupino Lane, British actor (b. 1892)
- November 15 – Charles Thomson Rees Wilson, Scottish physicist, Nobel Prize laureate (b. 1869)
- November 17 – Heitor Villa-Lobos, Brazilian composer (b. 1887)
- November 21 – Max Baer, American boxer and actor (b. 1909)
- November 22 – Molla Mallory, American tennis champion (b. 1884)
- November 24 – Dally Messenger, Australian rugby league player (b. 1883)
- November 25 – Gérard Philipe, French actor (b. 1922)
- November 29 – Hans Henny Jahnn, German playwright and novelist (b. 1894)

December

- December 4 – Hubert Marischka, Austrian film director (b. 1882)
- December 11 – Jim Bottomley, American baseball player (St. Louis Cardinals) and a member of the MLB Hall of Fame (b. 1900)

- December 14
  - Edna Wallace Hopper, stage actress (b. 1872)
  - Stanley Spencer, English painter (b. 1891)
- December 22 – Gilda Gray, Polish-born dancer and actress (b. 1901)
- December 23 – E. F. L. Wood, 1st Earl of Halifax, British politician (b. 1881)
- December 24 – Edmund Goulding, American director (b. 1891)
- December 28 – Ante Pavelic, Croatian fascist leader and WWII war criminal (b. 1889)

Nobel Prizes

- Physics – Emilio Gino Segrè, Owen Chamberlain
- Chemistry – Jaroslav Heyrovský
- Physiology or Medicine – Severo Ochoa, Arthur Kornberg
- Literature – Salvatore Quasimodo
- Peace – Philip Noel-Baker

In the News

The Guggenheim Museum designed by Frank Lloyd Wright in New York City is completed.

Mattel's Barbie Doll is Launched.

Fidel Castro comes to power in Cuba after Revolution with the first communist state in the west.

Alaska becomes the 49th State of the United States.

Hawaii becomes the 50th state.

The Luna 2 spacecraft crashes into the Moon to become the first man-made object on the Moon.

The Film Ben-Hur premieres in New York City.

NASA introduces America's first astronauts to the world including John H. Glenn Jr, and Alan Shepard Jr.

Southend Pier Pavilion is destroyed by fire.

An International agreement is signed to preserve Antartica.

Popular Films - Ben-Hur, Some Like It Hot, North by Northwest.

Popular TV Programmes - Bonanza, Juke Box Jury, Dixon of Dock Green (UK) The Huckleberry Hound Show.

The Dalai Lama is forced to flee Tibet.

1959 Calendar

January 1959

Sun	Mon	Tue	Wed	Thu	Fri	Sat
				1	2	3
4	5	6	7	8	9	10
11	12	13	14	15	16	17
18	19	20	21	22	23	24
25	26	27	28	29	30	31

February 1959

Sun	Mon	Tue	Wed	Thu	Fri	Sat
1	2	3	4	5	6	7
8	9	10	11	12	13	14
15	16	17	18	19	20	21
22	23	24	25	26	27	28

March 1959

Sun	Mon	Tue	Wed	Thu	Fri	Sat
1	2	3	4	5	6	7
8	9	10	11	12	13	14
15	16	17	18	19	20	21
22	23	24	25	26	27	28
29	30	31				

April 1959

Sun	Mon	Tue	Wed	Thu	Fri	Sat
			1	2	3	4
5	6	7	8	9	10	11
12	13	14	15	16	17	18
19	20	21	22	23	24	25
26	27	28	29	30		

May 1959

Sun	Mon	Tue	Wed	Thu	Fri	Sat
					1	2
3	4	5	6	7	8	9
10	11	12	13	14	15	16
17	18	19	20	21	22	23
24	25	26	27	28	29	30
31						

June 1959

Sun	Mon	Tue	Wed	Thu	Fri	Sat
	1	2	3	4	5	6
7	8	9	10	11	12	13
14	15	16	17	18	19	20
21	22	23	24	25	26	27
28	29	30				

July 1959

Sun	Mon	Tue	Wed	Thu	Fri	Sat
			1	2	3	4
5	6	7	8	9	10	11
12	13	14	15	16	17	18
19	20	21	22	23	24	25
26	27	28	29	30	31	

August 1959

Sun	Mon	Tue	Wed	Thu	Fri	Sat
						1
2	3	4	5	6	7	8
9	10	11	12	13	14	15
16	17	18	19	20	21	22
23	24	25	26	27	28	29
30	31					

September 1959

Sun	Mon	Tue	Wed	Thu	Fri	Sat
		1	2	3	4	5
6	7	8	9	10	11	12
13	14	15	16	17	18	19
20	21	22	23	24	25	26
27	28	29	30			

October 1959

Sun	Mon	Tue	Wed	Thu	Fri	Sat
				1	2	3
4	5	6	7	8	9	10
11	12	13	14	15	16	17
18	19	20	21	22	23	24
25	26	27	28	29	30	31

November 1959

Sun	Mon	Tue	Wed	Thu	Fri	Sat
1	2	3	4	5	6	7
8	9	10	11	12	13	14
15	16	17	18	19	20	21
22	23	24	25	26	27	28
29	30					

December 1959

Sun	Mon	Tue	Wed	Thu	Fri	Sat
		1	2	3	4	5
6	7	8	9	10	11	12
13	14	15	16	17	18	19
20	21	22	23	24	25	26
27	28	29	30	31